Time Will Show

ALSO BY PAM REHM

POETRY

The Larger Nature (Chicago: Flood Editions, 2011)
Small Works (Chicago: Flood Editions, 2005)
Gone to Earth (Chicago: Flood Editions, 2001)
To Give It Up (Los Angeles: Sun & Moon, 1995)
The Garment in Which No One Had Slept
(Providence: Burning Deck, 1993)

POETRY CHAPBOOKS

Saving Bonds (Woodside, NY: The Cultural Society, 2002)
Piecework (Stockbridge, MA: o·blek editions, 1992)
Pollux (Buffalo, NY: Leave Books, 1992)

Pam Rehm

Time Will Show

Shearsman Books

First published in the United Kingdom in 2018 by
Shearsman Books
50 Westons Hill Drive
Emersons Green
BRISTOL
BS16 7DF

Shearsman Books Ltd Registered Office
30–31 St. James Place, Mangotsfield, Bristol BS16 9JB
(this address not for correspondence)

www.shearsman.com

ISBN 978-1-84861-599-1

CONTENTS

Time Will Show

The heart is forever inexperienced.
Henry David Thoreau

A Matter of Days

There is an ache
in each of us

A remoteness

An unsettled absoluteness
that embraces no variant

In the end, it figures closely
to the self's semblance

Part caution
Part allure

It is distinctly
our vigilant core

Time Will Show

The contents of need
balance between
yesterday and no longer

In consciousness, we worry
In spirit, we are safe

In the obscure
corners
of living

wonder warbles
in a sturdy nest

Away from home,
you keep its influence

piece out the comfort
then turn off the light

All or Nothing
for Michael Gizzi

All or nothing

A simple premise
for the complexity
of existence

It exhorts the
present's pull

duels with
the hour's mind,
the day's body

Every day, the same
exchanging

sleep for waking

Patterns are
a natural phenomenon

Something you memorize
can be forgotten

You break your heart
over a sentence

Because daydreams can't heal
talking

What's the big deal?

Silence holds its own
head up

Without the heavy flesh

forgiveness is
that things grow

is why we are here
still

The difference between
a shadow and a body

is merely the immortality
of habits

It is interesting to note
extremes
Winter's slow give-over
to green

encompasses sidewalk plots
and trees

The sun burns, its
heat still out of reach

I walk as compensation
for my growing devotion
to fate

Children at play
in the street

Your "About Face"
over and over

until the day
grows late

The weight of the air
changes

The voice fades

A thunderstorm begins

Everything is between
what causes

or what follows

interference

Guided by the temporary
strategies of adaptation

my mind

finds openings
at dawn

The Shadow of a Mountain

Upstream, the current is shallow

Deftly turning them over,
I have observed
rock bottoms
like flowers

The flowing water carries
a leaf on its surface

Face the wind
let it wind through your shirtsleeves

Pine trees hold wings
until they rise and disappear

from your enchantment
Dragonfly jaws work sideways

side by side in a row
The way of engagement is slow

Snow sometimes hides it
in a boy's pockets or

a girl's kite
rising with the sun

So much splendor stuns
the grounds of my acquaintance

with rock bottom

A rocky road through
a picture-perfect day

In Plain Sight

Crows on the lake ice
making a racket. I'd

die of embarrassment
to be that

loud. Cloudless sky
over an early afternoon
landscape. The sun

does not warm
but blinds. Where
do you find your days

when the delight
of passion has waned?

In Plain Sight II

Guided by temporary
insights

Notice everything
Understand little

A dead possum
rolled onto her back

I imagine
peering into worlds
beyond human understanding

Think of low tide
And come closer

In Plain Sight III

Cast over sky that
doesn't break to
the possibility of light.

This way for a long
stretch of days
chills the inside
rooms. Mid-morning

gray with geese
wildly flapping. I
welcome summer's

humid decline
into fall. October has
its own way

with colors.
Cosmic wonder.
Before and after.

The Questions

for Robert Creeley

Living—
part trap
part rapt
ure
How to spring it
How to give
oneself up
to it

"The Difficult Ideal"

If you accept
fate's feats
you will be guided

Otherwise,
pulseless disguises
compete

We either give
or withhold
heartbeats

Salt in the Nose

Who isn't a
walking paradox
beside these headlines

Daily grind
Dusk, that last glimmer
of light smolders inside
these land-bound eyes

Grounds me

Sensation is a tension
to the mind's stasis

Sensation as attention
between the self

and the smell of a river
flowing both ways

Out into the World Again

Once in awhile February feels
more like my own body

But I am relieved to behold

the melting
of winter's quiet

the attar of overheated rooms
dispelled by spring's
revelling endorsement

Each year
the sun's arc grows

to the noise of birds
flooding the memory

with an appetite
for green

The recurrence of the sensual
is April's honor

to which we stand
At attention

Autumn

After the dog days
the long rays of
the sun are done
with harshness

Identity with reason
returns

The season is one
of spurning closeness

The birds leaving
The leaves dropping

The vastness of the sky
is what holds me

at ease

Winter is close

Winter is close
        and mateless

Night, pensive—
           pressed
Eyes, deep glens
of old thoughts

My pillow
        a moon vigil

Words fall and root
Words grow glorious bodies

Time's dearest deity
is desire
Desire, fervent and steadfast

Steadfast and eternal

Civil Twilight

Where we sleep,
under the absence of stars,
the signs are
contaminated

To rectify a renewal
is of our own accord

Stasis is a gulf
we can cross with thought

The scarlet tanager
reminds us
to adjust ourselves
to the cycles,
the seasons,
the perpetual scattering of light

It is a vigilance
of starless watching

This elegy

We keep oaths
to rectify a renewal
of life-like movements

Cross off the dates,
date our days

At base, we cultivate
a cycle of suspension

Suspended between
patience and language

between the street lights

and the dark nights

Lost inside

Thoughts

All It Can Be
for Whit Griffin

The best questions
          dropped out of school

Gratitude like a dog waiting

To protect its silence
          a stream tunes itself
              over time

Everything earned inside
          is hard to describe
              like prayer or reverence

I follow the quiet
          deeper into my daydream

Sometimes conflicting values are more approachable
than virtue

Human noise reduces bird habitat—
          imagine that
              happening in reverse

Marvelling is the view with few words

To have to measure up is a sad level
          it is beyond our hands

Walking resonates through the feet
        up into the mind

But how exactly do I describe to you the joy of finding
    a cricket in the bathtub—
        Like a wave of applause
        soaking through me like rain?

The Great Indoors

Two mechanical clocks
Two cats

Minute sensations
Solitary intimations

No sunrise awareness
just its circular likeness

In the hour hand
Nothing happens

A debate with Plato
about shadows, continuity,

the complications of fate
There is never a body

without movement
Adjusting the face

Standing, even
These subtle shifts

in perception
The ins and outs

of recurring light
of appetite

and its edge
The bread rising

There is no horizon
Just morning's quiet

practically desperate
for attention

Too Late

The wind has shaken
my writing day

The ground
printed with tracks, beckons

An outline of mountains,
memories

I wish I could erase
my window

I cannot see
so many months, years

The perpetual ink-filled
rotation

Deep in uncertainties,
tendencies, ordinary brokenness

I had a thought in a dream
I forgot to make use of

Encounters with Silence

Absence feels
an unusual magnitude

It abides

A semblance
so tenuously wrought
one memory could
destroy it

Forgetting holds the day
incoherently together

Heightened contrasts
Feelings with no content

Low comfort
Cheap regard

Your voice
now an echo

of the silence
you loved

What meaning is
no one can understand
alone

To hear, I walked
Then silence found

returning home

Doubt runs parallel
Belief surrounds

The wings of an egret
standing still

I marvel at the momentary

Light
held by its reflection

The current pulling forward

Night, a tall ceiling
That orients the heart

The sound of water falling on trees
A woodcutter's ax

How little use was made
of artifice

from midday to midnight
with its stars

buried in snow

I would have paid all my days
to be worthy of your interest

of your household words
as guidance

The sound of water
falling through spring

air, deep as our natures

Bared of regret

The Story of the Heart

for Donald Revell

The story of the heart
opens up absences

The lost circulations
of the heavens

The in-between speech
of the mind
overhearing itself

Each day
after the next

You know you are alive,
and yet

Intimacy varies
the deeper down
you get

The body and the soul becoming one
Enigma

The body of this world

To hold each day
in humility

A melody

The body is biblical
The soul, the urgency of meaning

The body of the story
is a lost body

Here or nowhere

Your soul is at a loss

You heave your mind
into the throws of thought

The in-between openings
of the heart

The meaning of the story is
You pursue it

Love
as well as its distillations

Between reality and the soul
A stone's throw

Absence makes the heart grow
closer

Each day after the next
You know you are alive and yet

The mind overhearing itself
is the story

It makes visible the way

you hold each day
intimately

In silence

Alone

Absence is biblical

A stone's throw ripple across
The body and this world

Love goes deeper down

Love Has Tangents

Fidelity to patience
is the theme
I have kindled
behind every effort

The apogee
The same thing
A different way
Day after day

My love has tangents
not resolutions

Times have changed
Time has changed

Passing into one another
The surface of gestures
An amalgam
of deepening touch

Abandon ideology
Abandon self-loss
The wager is visible

There is no difference
Between the damned and the saved

Pardon
An inseparable face
Inside you

There is always the tumult
Then a pursuit of reticence
The closing of a wound
Of cruelty and its intimate nicknames

One finds everything
Where future and past meet

Enough to disappear
Into the claims of the present

Talk

Mouth pressed to paper
Pressed to mouth

Sanctum

So much of our time
is an unequal distribution of feelings

Retrospection commiserates
with retrospection

But we remain mute
And the days come and go

the soul wanting no mouthpiece
to distinguish desire from happiness

We need only hold ourselves
poised—
as waiting is more than withstanding

It is the sanctum

After the evening's sun has escaped
into the night, its heat and light
still pulsating in the imagination

a tension exists between
intensity and duration

That tension is our religion

Love has a future tense

no matter how confounding
its vocabulary has become

Eden II

Back and forth
across the music

You, a sad Adam
Caught in the apple
in your eye

Inquiry reproached
A chastened passion

No longer
your keeper's keeper

The birds, wounded
A broken sun
set

You step carefully
through days

A garden lost

I hear sirens
in your heart

A Pierced Heart

Your resolution of loss
is days going forward

through the mystery

Life after life

The body of a body
Osiris

This vain solemnity
of loving

forged in language

Whatever hasn't crumbled
in the rush of systems,
of given limits

Coalesces
in the alchemy of living

Strange intimations
of definitions

Irrevocable alterations
From which

A coherence is regained

How to Mend a Friend

The growing and opening
beneath the ice
of the beating organ

will win
You know the sun
will come
like breathing

to carry on, so
Speak to no one
Walk over snowy tracks
Embrace an animal body

Distinguish between
a good sign and a stand-in
Follow a shadow
Name a higher figure

Attend to ordinary things

Divided Attention

Stuck on first pages

Fixed on months passing
No standards

A perverse impulse to pretend

Flush of the wind
Skepticism

Caught out in the multitudes

Penning "God help us"
after the lost plane and mudslides

No one wants to be missing
Just missed

Squeezed between
the beginning and ending
of the day's melodies

The body, the five faculties,
and impulse

Desire, a channel
that is always on—

a text you can close

like curtains

to all else—

Well-worn sarcasm
Well-worn questioning

I have the heart of a believer
The mind of a self-imposed rule

*

The Spirit lasts—but in what mode—

Emily Dickinson

The Sound of the Spirit

for my mother

One must adjust anguish
slowly to oneself
Grow into it
until the comfort is wearable

You do what you have to

Stop to watch the motion
of cold shadows
outside the bedroom window

I know it is more complicated—
this focus on the familiar
cycles of light

But what is the message
the truth expressed
except worn remembrance

The first thing you do
is get dressed

The second
go out on the back porch
and listen

The Shape of the Spirit

The shape of the spirit
shakes out
day length

Hair or a river bed
Walking after daybreak

If I should lose you
to yesterday
lingering in the ruins
of an old heart
Mine would be the
paltry fate

Habits make meaning
Caring makes us mortal

But what my mind has lost
without rituals
my heart has felt undeniably

A thin ghost
An exposed foothold

The bones of the trees
A tracery of starlings
skittering

The Silence of the Spirit

Down in the roots
Mysticism and mystery
close the eyes and the mouth

You are not yourself
You are an encounter
of concentration

Charting the hidden

At the heart of it
an inner tongue

An anointing
bewilderment

A poignant forfeit

A window landscape
before the rain moves in

The Desolation of the Spirit

We are all a consequence of
feral clarity

and the elements
of experience
more imagined than bestowed

In the immensity of the hour
by hour day
nothing is promised

Even falling in love
against doubt, is just
an angle of vision

The starting point
is always the same
morning search

My dreaming heart
a synthesis
as I think down
a dark world

Letting go of rescue
to be awakened
to duration

It is a fearful thing
to contemplate

Unfelt sorrow

The heart still beats, but
is it worthy?
Beside this pulsing Earth

You are trying to understand
crisis
The difference between
a shadow

and a body
without love in its veins

Damnation is relative
and so your name is not

emblematic of your being

At the edge of the void
the spirit is everything

The Needs of the Spirit

Detachment
is an emphasis

It lays bare the bones
to the experiment
within you

Every moment new

Here, is no oath

I walk alone

I went walking

I am afoot
to this frequency

Past presence

Every moment

To the ends
of it

The Strength of the Spirit

There are no external marks
It quickens into life and feeds

close to you
Extends itself into the sleeping hours

There is no reprieve
But a spreading wide

exercise in elucidation
A balance between guide and watchman

Step after step
in the thought of tomorrow

and tomorrow and
You are nothing more than

your own equalling of yourself
with yourself

Always and everywhere
Your own resurrection

The Testament of the Spirit

I consider my recognition
of myself

What does it evolve
What remains

A range of common sense
defying validation?

I consider chance
and what it affords

Resiliency
and what it verifies

I consider the body
inundated with necessities

incomprehensible emotions
I cannot sustain

Attention is the tonic
I locate the spirit in

Not discipline
Nor intuition

But an immeasurable vigilance

At every moment
I suffer myself
to be beckoned

*

Even at attention
a poet's faith
can quieten

Too many
cold-shoulder walks
for anyone

So quiet
must become prayer

So prayer must become
walking

So walking
must become continuing

Alongside intervals
Alongside ghostly imperatives

Too much to shoulder

Even at attention
A poet's quiet
can quieten

A notional faith
A walking restitution

Acknowledgments

Heartfelt thanks to the editors of *Colorado Review, the cultural society, The Doris, Jubilat,* and *Seedings* for publishing some of these poems.

My deepest thanks to Nate, Cora, and especially to Lew. This is for you.

Notes

'The Shadow of a Mountain' takes its title from this entry in Thoreau's journal: "It were as well to be educated in the shadow of a mountain as in more classical shades."

'Winter is Close' takes its words from Emily Brontë's poem 'Faith and Despondency.'

'Love Has Tangents' was written after seeing Arnaud Desplechin's beautiful, beautiful film *My Golden Days*.

'The Difficult Ideal' is a line from Emily Dickinson's poem #750.

The Author

Pam Rehm is the author of *The Larger Nature, Small Works, Gone to Earth, To Give It Up,* and *The Garment in Which No One Had Slept.* She lives in New York City.

CPSIA information can be obtained
at www.ICGtesting.com
Printed in the USA
FSHW02n0131131018
52895FS